A Beautiful Catastrophe

A Beautiful Catastrophe

Poems

Murray Dunlap

RESOURCE *Publications* · Eugene, Oregon

A BEAUTIFUL CATASTROPHE
Poems

Copyright © 2020 Murray Dunlap. All rights reserved. Except for brief quotations in critical publications or reviews, no part of this book may be reproduced in any manner without prior written permission from the publisher. Write: Permissions, Wipf and Stock Publishers, 199 W. 8th Ave., Suite 3, Eugene, OR 97401.

Resource Publications
An Imprint of Wipf and Stock Publishers
199 W. 8th Ave., Suite 3
Eugene, OR 97401

www.wipfandstock.com

PAPERBACK ISBN: 978-1-7252-6258-4
HARDCOVER ISBN: 978-1-7252-6259-1
EBOOK ISBN: 978-1-7252-6260-7

Manufactured in the U.S.A.   02/12/20

The author gratefully acknowledges the editors for the following publications where the poems first appeared.

- "Birth," *Episcopal Café Magazine*
- "An Imperfect Brain" and "Hope," *Ability Magazine*
- "Perfection," "The Voices Project"
- "Confession," *Hope Magazine*

Remember not the former things, nor consider the things of old. Behold, I am doing a new thing; now it springs forth, do you not perceive it? I will make a way in the wilderness and rivers in the desert.

—ISAIAH 43:18–19

The wreck was certainly catastrophic, but where it led me is nothing but beautiful. I would like to dedicate this book to anyone who endures a traumatic brain injury. After it is all said and done, this book should prove that there is hope.

—MURRAY DUNLAP

Contents

Birth   1
I Am on My Way   2

   What If   5
   Transit   7
   The Devil Blew In   8
   The Way   9
   A Life Unhinged   10
   Words   11
   The Blue Hyacinth in Trust   12
   The Passionate Ones   13
   Hope   14
   Deprivation   15
   The Natural Now   16
   The Weight   17
   Peace   18
   Rebirth of Cool   19
   Leavened   20
   Disability   21
   Stealing Identity   22
   Traffic   23

Crying Out	24
Vacuous Void	25
Amnesia	26
Forgiveness	27
Defining Beautiful	28
The Answer	29
Under the Guise	30
Her Power	31
Define Yourself	32
Go	33
A Traumatic Life	34
We Dance	35
Devil in the Details	36
This South	37
Here and Now	38
Bracelets	39
Strategy	40
Photograph	41
Help	42
Anticipation	43
Division	44
Heart of a Flatline	45
Church of the Resurrection Episcopal	46
My Own Body	47
Inoculate God	48
Chaos	49
Suddenly	50
Decisions	51
Empirical Thoughts	52

Judge Fire	53
An Angel Arrived	54
Key	55
Chance	56
In Truth	57
Restore	58
Forward Movement	59
Patience	60
Move	62
An Imperfect Brain	63
Come Clean	64
Perfection	65
Confession	66
Afterword: Thank you, Ed	67

Birth

THE OLD MAN sat Indian style with cupped hands. From a distance, he appeared to be rubbing his hands together for warmth. At a closer range, it was clear that he held something. Perhaps a firefly. The firefly would blink its light, and the old man would put his mouth to his hands and blow. The light grew with the old man's breath. And then he did the most spectacular thing. He opened his hands and the light stayed put. This was not a firefly. The orb remained constant. Tiny specs seemed to circle the orb in extremely particular ways. The old man appeared pleased. He spoke aloud to the air around him, "Keep them warm, my little orb, and we will name you Sun. I will send my own son when you are constant enough to keep him safely warm."

And so, our universe was born.

I Am on My Way

"The hardest thing I have been asked is to describe what a brain injury is. It is impossible to describe brain injury. Imagine a hurricane, a tornado, a tsunami. It destroys everything in an instant. You are expected to start over and stay positive while doing so. Brain injury is learning to walk a tight rope between hope and being realistic. Both are equally important. Finding the right balance is a daily struggle."

HSF (A TRAUMATIC BRAIN INJURY SUPPORT GROUP)

    A man's life had changed in the twitch of his dreaming eye. A waterfall of thoughts, decisions, and understanding cascaded over a cliff and collected in the pond below. The information was still there, twirling about in the collected water, but there was no rhyme or reason to any method of fishing it out. The man felt his life was over. And his old life was. He lost his first wife and his ability to write the prose he had dreamed of.
    A former fiction writer, he now wrote poetry. A former distance runner, he now hobbled along, mostly walking. In his past life, his memory was strong. Now, amnesia. He had 3 fractures in his pelvis, a broken clavicle, 9 sutures in his head, five stitches in his ear, and a traumatic brain injury . . .

So, this man started a new life. Married a new girl. Found a new path. It hardly resembled what had driven him to graduate school in California where he had married on the beach. Now he was driven to teach himself poetry. Now he married a priest. Now the long-term goals had become elusive, so he is driven to make the most of every single day.

He is driven to embrace the moment, in whatever form that takes.

I am that man, and I tell you to **embrace the now.** In a twitch of your dreaming eye, it could vanish. Do not live for tomorrow. Live for today.

If I believed in myself, this would all be moot. With a traumatic brain injury, I am not sure what I believe anymore. My reality has changed in profound ways over a decade. I went from this to that, but you don't want to know. The reality is where I find myself now, and it is a beautiful place, full of grace and love. My failure to believe in myself lies somewhere else. In the dark and hidden places that I reveal only when I am alone in the impossibly early hours. In these bleak hours, I try to find the courage to submit my writing for publication to places vastly beyond my scope. I hope to somehow get a lucky break, and be allowed to say, 'see, this is what I do with the time allowed by not working a job.'

My truth infuriates me. I rely on the hope for a lucky break to grant myself a vague sense of peace. At 45, I believe in God and a dim hope for a lucky break.

I don't have any real friends and am quite sure that I am the definition of insanity.

Today, all of the above changes. My primary care doctor gave me a sleeping pill regimen that actually works. For the first time in 10 long years, I can sleep. With renewed energy, I will refocus on my art and poetry and generally, live a fuller, happier life. Failing at regular sleep is an indescribable torture. Finally relearning to sleep is a winning lottery ticket. It seems plausible, in fact, that I will believe in myself -rendering ***anything*** possible.

I had been somebody. Not there yet, but I was writer blooming. Finished graduate school with Pam Houston. Begun publishing short stories in literary journals. Married the hot girl from high school. Had been offered a job teaching English and creative writing at a prestigious high school.

I had been on my way.

Then catastrophe struck like lightning. With no premonitions, a nice fellow missed a red light and all of the above was put on hold. A 3-month coma. A year in a wheelchair. A traumatic brain injury. A writer would be finished right? That 1st marriage was. And that teaching offer. That wasn't taken away exactly, but I was a man gone mad.

I had written a book before my wreck. Published that after, but to no great acclaim. Wrote another book of short stories and published that, but to even less publicity. My 3rd book, well, that caught eyes. I had started writing poetry and found myself on the news for a half an hour.

But all that said, it felt like pity given to the guy with a brain injury. Like I was entitled to acclaim for my disabled work. Just typing that sentence makes me furious without reprieve.

I had come along in other ways. I had remarried. This time, a beautiful priest. I could even jog, albeit in my strange limping/walking way. I lost fifty pounds. And at a fine fighting weight, I wrote another book. This one was called *A Beautiful Catastrophe*. Poetry again, but with pace and maturity. My new book will be published by Wipf and Stock this year.

Now I wait. Now I jog. Now I smile. And now I write better poetry, make better art, and generally have a better attitude about life. I may be broken, but I am a man in bloom.

I am on my way.

What If

What if I could suspend
Reality for grace
What if I could put
Violence on hold
What if I could redirect
Passion and love
To the place it is needed
Now

What if I could skip
Backward in time
What if I could make
A safer call
What if I could wait
For my angel to appear
Hold everything
Upon a drop of water

What if my present time
Confounds all
What if my occupation
Is fearless
What if I am a new man
Entirely
And the misdirected anger
Goes quiet
And still
And the greater love fills
My need to be complete

While you may not see it
I am complete
A new man
A new life
A new world
I measure my grace
In unseen ways

Call me now
Retire your dreams
Take on the new
Completed man

What if

Transit

The gentleman in the black suit paid his bill, made for the door, and cried

The lavender dress on the girl at his table tore when she stood

Significant details fill my leaden mind

I dive deep in thought while in transit

The man in the black suit had inquired why

Lavender girl simply stared with her over-sized, teary blue eyes

'Why have you come to me?'

'You are my father.'

I carry these conversations as some carry a leather briefcase

I carry them in transit as dirty flies hitch a ride

The man in black worried he had failed his daughter

He had not known he had one

Lavender girl had only recently been told

She only hoped to connect

I search my brain but I am not sure

Why did I tell her?

I pace my transit

The Devil Blew In

In bending metal
And broken glass
He grabbed my brain
And squeezed
My academics, gone
My common sense, wounded
When the Devil blew in
And purloined my IQ
I forfeited everything I had

My high school sweetheart, lost
My teaching career, disabled
My ambition, slowed
But not stopped
God won that battle
And brought me back to relevance

On the news, twice
Wrote three new books
Relearned to walk
To speak clearly
To sleep
To think
To love

I am here to win
Yes, it took a decade
But I am back
And I want more
I will be triumphant

This is my alternate ending:
I speak to crowds, not just students
I jog every day, not wheelchair-bound
I married a priest, not a memory
Confident, at last
I thumb my nose at the devil

The Way

Tattered waves
Nausea
Then epiphany
The birth of a thought

Magnetic attachment
Desire
True love
The birth of a marriage

Clarity of mind
Peaceful philosophy
Controlled sedation
The birth of a peace

Tireless devotion
Speaking to crowds
Standing ovation
The birth of a new life

Once down
Now alive
Once out
Now fierce

In the depths, I found my path
Between words, I found hope
Through my wife, I found God
This is the way

A Life Unhinged

Having been jeopardized
Tossed about on four wheels
Then met the devil
All left me wanting
Endeavoring truth
I descend to kiss
The metal of solid ground
The permanence of work
The permanence of love
The decisions we make
In an impermanent world

Do look above
And decide:
Trust in God

Words

I believe in words
The power to move you
To persuade you to my need
The words, a micro-bit thin, and a fixed number of colors and shades
A flat panel monitor, the thinnest
The words escape my reality
In truth, they seem not to exist
But the power, so grand
You will be moved
In the words, you coerce me right back

I believe in words

The Blue Hyacinth in Trust

Under the spell
I am paralyzed by beauty
I am breath-taken by love
I am wordless

The spell is broken and I fall
But then I stand straight
Again, I am paralyzed by beauty
I am breath-taken by love
And I am wordless

The Blue Hyacinth before me stands tall after everything
Her unbreakable spine, flexed with love

She said yes, so I walked down the aisle to her
Then of course, I said yes too
Nothing is compromised
We are wordless, still

My Hyacinth purges our wants
For our needs with sincerity
She is in trust
A partnership with God
Eliciting happiness

Wordless, we smile

The Passionate Ones

Little by little
They surpass
mounting our fears
And triumph
They are the passionate ones
The little angels who storm
Our lives inspired for positivity
For good

Racing little devils
Clawing out the bad

Commit now
You have passion
You decide your life
With the angels on our shoulders
We triumph
We triumph, ourselves
Now

Hope

There is hope
Shown at the end of a torturous path
View it with the Ability
Given by the endurance of strength
And the grace of God

Almost super-human
Our ability to endure
Turn around
And take more

The display is effortless
The well-timed Ability
The showcase of our fears
Imbedded in hope

My prayer is elegant
From the found to the lost:
Kneel, pray, and hope

Deprivation

Sometimes
If I haven't slept in a few days
The edges of my reality blur
Into a sort of hyper-real, malleable
Depth of truth
On these days I stay low
Maintaining a sense of self
Follow outward rules of society
But my brain goes places it should not
I stop reality on its head
I find that place of comfort
Where I do not have a disability
Where I can walk true
Where I speak clearly without error
Where my conscience knows truth

But the fact is I am disabled
I misspeak often
I walk with a limp
And I am often wrong

This is my time of learning
But soon I will have
A license to smile

When I cannot sleep
I follow my heart

The Natural Now

Slight
That comfort of comprehension
That steady balance
In an instant
It was gone

Fast
The start of love
The weariness to reenter
That imperative balance
Leaping into reality
Dive

Believe
The illusion evaporates
The reality, the truth
Intoxicating with happiness
So strong, so true
Balanced
Now

The Weight

The weight of me
Coming at you right now
Do you see me, right now
Unfolding my soul
Into your arms
Seeing the blackness
Enveloping white
Right now, it is welcome
Right now, it is pure
The weight of my storming brain
Riding a wall
The weight of my forward motion
Pulling you along
In fact, my weight
Compels you to cry
To walk away
Just look, right now
It is the weight

Peace

The system has changed -only for you
Your brain has been compromised
And nothing is as it once was, or should be
Your balance, your body, your brain
A beautiful catastrophe
You are lost, and yet, found
A miracle of events has given you
A perfect, delicate peace
Punctuated by pain
But a peace, nonetheless
We all strive for peace

Rebirth of Cool

After cool is born
I died in a car wreck
Tickling tubes of motion
Pushed to cement below

Effortless before I died
Cool became impossible
Walk with a limp
And speak with a slur

Cool comes back into view
By writing
A timid tundra
Etched small

Enlarge the canvas
A boisterous affair
Reach an audience
Beyond anticipation

The engraved invitation
To be cool

Leavened

I stand before you
I hold the column for balance
I am unsure of what to say
Or how to say it
Yes, I am standing
But will tire soon and sit
The world changed, for me
In the broad strokes of recovery

I am unsure
I am without confidence
I am unable to do so many things

That understood
I wrote a book of poetry
I married a priest
On most days
I am happy

Despite being ill equipped
I am grateful
I am leavened
I have relearned to smile

Disability

The world is upon us
We listen for truth
Careening toward death
But slowing for peace

Feel slackening hands
Paced without time
A nostalgic glance
Tightening our thoughts

Bursting from stale
Thrust forward with speed
We may be disabled
But in matters of grace
We hold this win

Stealing Identity

My life went awry
In that very instant
Timed to the split second
Without my heart
Indefinite conclusion and
Lost identity
A vagrant continued life
Iron weights in my pockets
Cement in my shoes

I journey on
I find respite
In the life of another
Stolen from photographs
Interpretation
Now

Traffic

In life, we spend time waiting
As kind ones, we wait for others to turn
To pass
To stop and park
As in life, we set out for personal gain
To get there faster
To get the best parking

We can intersect, at times, with others on a path
To bend metal and break glass
To evacuate our path for another
Remember now: others' path is important to them
That they must reach their destination
In spite of yours

We all are moving
Pushing ourselves ahead
But our path is not the only way to get there
And we are not the only ones going

Finally, we find parking
On a soft passing cloud
We turn off vehicles
Let our engines cool
And shake hands with old friends
From another path
A lifetime away

Crying Out

Crying out for peace
I find myself sore
Beaten
Exhausted

Crying out for sanity
I find myself perplexed
Deceived
Lost

Crying out for a little love
I find myself inadequate
Undeserving
Unable to repay

Crying out for Truth
I find myself believing
Saved
I find myself on my knees

Vacuous Void

The terrific imbalance of my brain
Not the imbalance of my body
Not steps, nor stairs
But the vacuous void I fill with prattle
My 'work' is a joke
My joke -so complex, I made the news
'Poor guy,' they say
Pity that man
I create art as 'work'
When the word 'correct' is impossible to define
This is where I coast
My home
The vacuous void

Amnesia

We unwilfully extract parts of our lives
We cannot remember
Devastatingly vacuous appendages
Of our bodies
Dissection by virtue
Implementation of a ghost
What we cannot remember
We destroy

Forgiveness

With bottomless anger
And other-worldly frustration
Comes a ring to be free
Less aimless direction
Less self-destruction
More heart
More love

The magic spell,
Spoken aloud:
"I forgive you"

Defining Beautiful

Waking from a coma, fragile or not
Stepping from a wheelchair, despite the falls
Surviving a scalding divorce
Learning a new skill, in a new town
Meeting a priest to marry
Publishing a new book
To be asked on the news

Learning to define yourself
In a positive way

From the deepest darkness to the impossible light
After ten years of grueling work
Beautiful

The Answer

Within my cognitive wheels
Turns an answer
Inside my soul
Appears a vision
You are the single finest element
To round my life
And bring my ethics into focus
Our love makes me whole
Our love purifies my heart
Our love equates riches
Our love is the answer

Under the Guise

Bleeding identity
Timeless motions
Startling belief
Smile

Anonymous presence
Feeling the freedom
A life unknown
Under the guise
Happiness

Again
We smile

Her Power

Hurricane Florence
Lost power first thing
An electric life: disconnected
Email friends and family, no more
Laptop movies, gone
Phone charge lost
But that sparkle in her eye
And beautiful skin
At the curve of her spine
An electricity of her own
Feelings remain
And the power of hearts
An endless reserve

Florence crawls
But passes at last
And the new power source
Her heart
Is imbedded in his mind
Losing electricity can be overcome
When the fuel of the heart
Steers us true

Define Yourself

Edges of sadness
Ineloquent needs
Timid at best
The accident was real
Without memory

Where do I belong?
Who have I become?
Refuse definition
But ask, am *I* real?

Connect with another
Begin to belong
Love and pray
The answer is yes

Go

Your birthday' eve
Reorganizing thoughts
10 years since the wreck
But tomorrow, gone
Whittled from insanity
Tireless energy, anew
Working for more

Your wife, your guide
Your everlasting wife
10 years vanish
Take your wife's hand
And start the hell over

Tomorrow, life plus one
The marriage of a lifetime
Revamp your gears
And go

A Traumatic Life

Brain injury equates
Perpetual anxiety
Constant fear
Am I doing this right?
Are you happy?
Are you satisfied?

Am *I* happy?
No answer
Just echoes down a musty hallway

We get quiet
We become still
Our relief is
Mute

Tomorrow may have an answer
Until then
We are mute

We Dance

At once
Change the world
Next
Change the heart
Illuminate
Our ways of living
Illuminate
Truth
Carve the path
Embrace faith
Crave the light
We are dancing with God

Devil in the Details

Tempted by the little things
When life gets so big
Learn to walk again
But miss the smile
So you superglue your teeth together
At Lucifer's claim
Passing driver's rehab
But live in mother's garage

His dark presence
Looms on the edges of your life
So you marry a priest
And all bets are off

With love's wings
You defy and triumph
The details are corrected
You move to North Carolina
And relearn to smile

This South

Grew up in Alabama
Then explored the world
A wreck disabled me
So I staggered home

This South was waiting
Despite virulent trauma
Disabled, but healing
I call it home

Anxious to live
This South is a spring-board
From which I catapult
My brain is traumatic
A life on pause

But from this South
I careen fearless
New art, new life
Invest in divinity
Relearn to smile

Acutely aware
Of my tenuous place
This South holds me

Here and Now

When a coma was my state
Nothing was possible
When a wheelchair came into play
Nothing was probable
When a priest came into my life
All bets were off
Words came back to my brain
And action followed
Books were born
In defiance

Reaching a bigger sense of peace
Living and loving life
Right here
Right now

Bracelets

I needed a bracelet
Adorned with cross
With necklaces came rash
Any noises drove me mad
Clicking and ticking

It had to shower after a jog
It had to stay put, waterproof
The cadence of my sweaty stride

My love for God had to travel
Could not set off metal detectors
Could not hook other bags
Could not slow me down

I could not find what I needed
So I made one
It took over fifty tries
Too loose; too tight; too shiny; too bright
Clicking and ticking
The crosses might be too big; too heavy

Finally, my silent little cross
Tied with a knot
Waterproof and light
Just right

But my love for Christ
Resides right in my heart
It doesn't make a sound
Even waterproof, of course
Having been there
The entire time

Strategy

Patience
So difficult
Marinate efforts
Let your work shine
Stop making problems
Start learning the goal
Given the time
All will be revealed

You've done the work
Effort pays off
In time
Dividends of love
God steps in

Photograph

Christ is wrought with pain in the foreground
His hands pierced, His tightened muscles burn
In the background, an older priest
Her wrinkled face etched with worry
Her closed eyes show meditation
Fear and concern
But Christ is close
His arms may tremble
But His heart sings
Not what she expects, but in other ways
Her prayers are answered

Help

Lord, please help me
Yes, you saved me
You created a man from broken bones
Broken brain
You gave me an angel for my wife
Lord, you saved me
You gave me strength
But if you could, please tell me what to do
Please direct my actions beyond rambles
My inadequate comprehension
My word, I am lost
Lord, please tell me where to go
Tell me what to say
Tell me who to tell
Lord, I am yours
A puppet at your bidding
My God, was I spared for a reason?
Yes Lord, You saved me
What now?

Anticipation

Her scent drifts over from an adjacent table
Her name is called, so you learn it
'Paula,' a tall man shouts. 'Double latte for Paula?'
With large brown eyes, she looks up, stands, and retrieves her coffee

You watch everything happen
The cleavage when she pushes off the table to stand
The rise of her skirt when she returns
Her scent, above all, lingers after her pass

Inventing reason to speak
You announce her napkin dropped
She takes your offer
Fingertips just touching

'Are you here alone?'
She asks
'Not anymore . . .'
You respond

The energy in the room
Palpable

Division

We argued.
'You think a judge is going to believe you and your brain injury?'
As it turned out, he did.
A signature worth a million dollars.
Sympathy doled out, just the same.
The earned peace:
A good night's sleep.

Heart of a Flatline

Electrical system intact
But suddenly
Electricity disorganized
Insidious lack of oxygen
Electrical patterns dive
Inadequate love
Rapid and inefficient rhythm
Drops rapidly to dangerously low levels
Now arouse ventricular fibrillation
Chaotic contractions
Esoteric fighter
Physiologically speaking
But, in the absence of any activity
Cardiac arrest
Let go
Flatline

Church of the Resurrection Episcopal

I was on a worn path
Tried and true
But tragedy struck as a devil's spell
Leaving me weak and foolish

Then I took a different path
With light, swift feet
Under God's direction
I made my way to a new identity
A resurrection of my own

A new wife
A new book
A new outlook on life

Follow His word
Breathe His air
Touch His creation

I am reborn in this world
A servant of God

My Own Body

I had been whole
Then a car went off-course
My brain went numb
And I left my own body

I had been smart
Written a book
But I left my own body

Traveling through time
The past is lost
And I left my own body

Relearning to smile
Relearn the dance
I left my own body

Reaching for a hand
Reaching for love
Reaching to remember
My own body

Cement holding
The best possible fit
For my own body

Inoculate God

We are fleas, my brother
A plague upon this earth
We employ torture
His son proved that truth
But our tendency for war:
His nuclear antidote
In our silence
Lies His grace

We can't prove a thing
So keep right on singing, sisters
Embrace your faith
And love life

Perhaps God would approve

Chaos

For an OCD man like me
It might surprise you
That chaos is my religion

Neat, clean, tidy to a fault
But only now can this exist
Hospitals, never ending nurses
Doctors upon doctors
Chaos was bestowed upon my life
On my very brain
Without choice, I came to accept it

Chaos is my religion
A brother of Christ
With the blood of chaos, nonetheless
Suspension of my disbelief
Chaos

Suddenly

For us all
Life is interrupted
A dire consequence of random acts
Hearts moved
But
Time to amend
Time to heal
Time to start over

Arrogance is alleviated
By the calm of pain
Forced meditation
The horizon of truth

Pick up your keys
Take exit
Balance your soul
And love

Decisions

In a time of heavy decisions
And long nights spent deep
My life changed without thought
My entire world combed inside out
Without a moment of plan

I stand before you in awe
Of the changes made
The turns taken
The plans are gone

Instead, my life:
A reaction
A reconfigured twin
An old photograph, reframed

But the parts have been fixed
The mess cleaned up
The elegant solution
To a chaotic equation
A monumental wreck

I live as you watch
Fresh and new
I stretch my tired muscles
And I burn through the anger
The depression and hate

I've relearned to love
Please see my heart
I have decided
It is ready for you

Empirical Thoughts

Without words
We do not exist
A slanderous remark
Demands volume
In silence
We stand alone

Provoking thoughts
Take words for launch
Truly believe
And you will shout
In terror, remark
In peace, speak the truth

These thoughts are our own

Judge Fire

Melting in place
Timed in degrees
Blackened deeply with soot
The heat turned inward
With lost logic
Impending truth

In the cooling days of fall
Cool and wet
Disorderly guilt
Extinguishing passion
Tempestuous heart
Sharpened claws
Loveless

Judge Fire presides
The verdict: divorce
Flames leaping joyous

White hot justice
Radiant heat
Burn

An Angel Arrived

The traumatic life
With memory unhinged
Muddled heart
Broken body
Misdirected mind

Yet divine corrections
An angel arrived
Hope

Key

A continuous monologue
To free my soul
Unleash it
Imprisoned within
Bending metal and broken glass

There is a key
In the shape of a heart
Rectify the words
Bequeath meaning
The key is marriage

The word is love

Chance

The market had crashed
Taylor lay his head on his desk
The pistol sat in a side drawer

Ella walked in
Perspiration glazed her face
'The numbers cannot be right!'
She shouted
Taylor did not move
Ella cleared her mind
'Dinner, the Boaz?'

Impossible time passed
Taylor lifted his head and smiled
'The Boaz gave up. They closed for good.'
Ella's face curled in anger
'The Boaz died, as we all are dying.'
Taylor removed the pistol and held it

The Police decided it was a double suicide
Smoke still hung in the air when they arrived
Until they read Taylor's note

Ella was cheating
Make her pay
I'll pay too

The obituary read as a fairy tale

The beautiful, young couple had often dined at Boaz
Where they discussed investing strategy
They left nothing to chance

They had emptied their accounts
Leaving nothing to anyone
Chance was the least of their concern

In Truth

In truth, I have loved twice
Most say you are lucky to love once

My first love was interrupted
By bending metal and broken glass

My second love is a graceful place to heal
Where I would prefer to live out my days

The truth about love
Is the honesty of motion
We do not stand still

So we love the right heart
At the right time

With changes
In truth, we move

Restore

Crowds, exposure
The fast lane
Error
Honest silence
Immediate response
Ambulance

Transition
Walking anew
Honest love
Walking the aisle
The fast lane
Restore

Forward Movement

In dire need of validation
In dire need of hope
We spin our gears in tedious plays to gain forward movement
Profit, security, sanity, love
We hope for more
And more
But we backpedal in times of conflict
In times lacking grace
We pray for resolution
We pedal forward for profit, security, sanity, love
We evolve into grinding wheels
Our forward motion gives the illusion
Of hope
And productivity
One more time

Patience

There have been so many dogs

Lumbering through my life

And the one quality

They (and most dogs) lacked:

Patience

My memory reminds me of one dog

Who was altogether different

Owen possessed patience

I limp, I stumble

But Owen would wait

And wait

Owen did not cry

Did not bark

He waited, with perfect poise

I fight gravity daily

And Owen would wait

Once, a squirrel caught Owen acting like a dog

And he felt shame

His head between his paws

Of the multitude, Owen embodied patience

But, in time, our son passed

And we took his ashes to the family plot

We'll join him again one day

But until then, Owen patiently waits

Move

Movers in
Movers out
Big, heavy items
Light, spurious details
All clenched within a giant truck

We move to a church
The town is secondary
I married a priest
Our life is Episcopal

We keep all in play
Until hitting the truck
Then we pray
Silently, but with hope

I am distracted by my book
Out for consideration
Seeking publication
Is like having faith

We close our eyes
And pray
That my words *might* find purchase
And our knees *will* find an altar
For in God we trust
In words, I hope

An Imperfect Brain

I define myself through curved glass
With my wife, I feel permitted to smile
If my brain allows, I communicate
When it does not, meditation
I spiral inward upon the reality
Recovery does not exist

The days are traumatic
As time warbles on
Stop
Even through a curve
This love is real

Come Clean

I was smart once
Years ago
But coma, wheelchair, and brain injury
Have led me astray
The things I took for granted
Countless and gone

I held a winning hand
Then a new dealer cut the deck
And I started to lose
I threatened to fold
But another dealer joined us
In the nick of time
And now
Straight aces

I come clean and admit
I am not as smart
But
From the second dealer, a winning hand
The dealer:
God

Perfection

In a new world with a new life
I toss the bent metal and broken glass behind me
I defy the car wreck defining me
Put me on the news, but did not steal my soul
Broke my brain, but did not limit my reach
My work is new
My outlook is fresh
I am disabled, but full of love
Thundering need for more
An unsatisfying wheelchair
So I jog every day
An unsatisfying life
So I married a priest
Now, now, now
Perfect

Confession

I've made mistakes
Some trivial
Some grave

I have caused pain
When it was unwanted
Unneeded

I have endured pain
Both unwilling
And unaware

I have run
Far and fast
Just to get away

So much has happened
So much has passed
Believe me now

My brain injury is real
My confession:
It was *not* my fault

Afterword: Thank You, Ed

I HAVE SAID *thank you* to Ed a number of years ago for 'leading me down the strange path that led to meeting my wife.' So, I've done that. Check. But, not in a way that would make Ed truly appreciate the gratitude I have for the vast number of ways my life has improved through my marriage to an Episcopal priest.

So, let me start over, Ed. First you must understand that my first wife was lovely, but neither one of us were equipped to reconcile with the amnesia that took our 5 years of marriage away from me, permanently. I cannot remember one bit of our wedding on a beach, nor our honeymoon, and worse, I was failing at pretending to understand. That ended our marriage and led me down the demonstrably dangerous path of living on my own and dabbling with online dating. I'll leave that story out for the obscenities that would be needed to explain. By the grace of God, I survived. The End.

The truth is, I am a better man, for everything I have been through. I have been to the bottom, and sure, some people have hypothetically been there, but I really was on my hands and knees, the bitter smell of a chemical burn, the eye watering sting of ammonia, there on the bottom. I have really been there. Not a hint of arrogance in my bones. Not an itch for fame and fortune. I want to be healthy. I want to be safe. When it is all said and done, I am a better man.

And better, I found and dated a girl just out of seminary, all prepared for a life serving God, and then I got down on one knee in the Alabama Bishop's office and -with his permission, asked her to spend the rest of her life with me, because well, with the bad comes the good. From devils to angels, I sputtered back to life, brain injury and all.

Ed, at this point you may be wondering what in the hell I brought you into this for. I'll remind you, Ed, that if it were not for your error, I would not have found my wife -and the writing life that has gone along with it.

Personally, I think my new book of poetry is the best thing I have written, before or after the brain injury. I call it *A Beautiful Catastrophe* and have high hopes for where it may take me.

The hard part to comprehend here, the true magic, is that I want to thank, and hell, I want to *embrace* the very man who put me in a 3-month coma. A year in a wheelchair. The very same man who gave me a severe traumatic brain injury. From which I recover a tiny bit, every single day.

Like everyone, my wife and I have our failings and shortcomings, but at the end of every day, she curls into me, we kiss, say I love you, and wish each other a great night's sleep.

This is all possible because a very nice man was distracted, missed a red light, and pushed me into oncoming traffic.

Thank you, Ed, thank you.

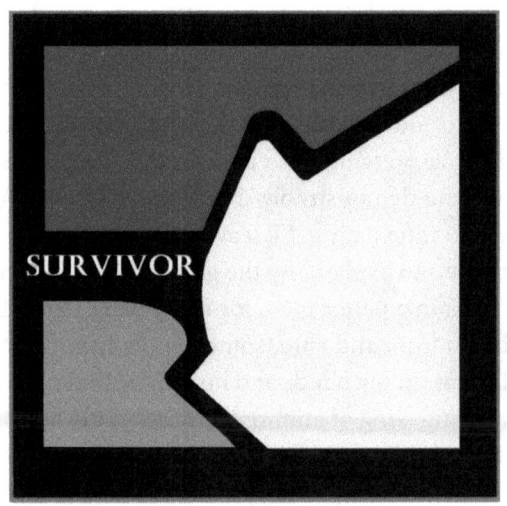

www.ingramcontent.com/pod-product-compliance
Lightning Source LLC
Chambersburg PA
CBHW071742040426

42446CB00012B/2442